TRIO

T0158459

THE HUGH MACLENNAN POETRY SERIES

Editors: Allan Hepburn and Carolyn Smart

TITLES IN THE SERIES

Trio

Sarah Tolmie

McGill-Queen's University Press
Montreal & Kingston • London • Ithaca

© McGill-Queen's University Press 2015
 ISBN 978-0-7735-4511-3 (paper)
 ISBN 978-0-7735-9702-0 (ePDF)
 ISBN 978-0-7735-9703-7 (ePUB)

Legal deposit first quarter 2015
Bibliothèque nationale du Québec

Printed in Canada on acid-free paper that is 100% ancient forest
free (100% post-consumer recycled), processed chlorine free

McGill-Queen's University Press acknowledges the support
of the Canada Council for the Arts for our publishing
program. We also acknowledge the financial support of the
Government of Canada through the Canada Book Fund
for our publishing activities.

The following is a work of fiction. Any resemblances
to individuals are purely coincidental.

Library and Archives Canada Cataloguing in Publication

Tolmie, Sarah, 1971–, author
  Trio / Sarah Tolmie.

  Issued in print and electronic formats.
  ISBN 978-0-7735-4511-3 (pbk.).
  ISBN 978-0-7735-9702-0 (ePDF).
  ISBN 978-0-7735-9703-7 (ePUB)

  1. Love poetry, Canadian (English). 2. Sonnets, Canadian
  (English). I. Title.

  PS8639.045T75 2015   C811'.6   C2014-906883-2
                                        C2014-906884-0

This book was typeset by Interscript in 9.5/14 New Baskerville.

.

For sonnet writers of all times and places,
but especially Wyatt, Shakespeare, Sidney, and Donne

TRIO

I

1

We're a trio; I hear your dusty feet
That I've never seen, dancing us round.
I imagine them, beautiful like your hands.
Man, woman, man, the two of you – and me,
Comedy central. Yet not farcical,
No misstep on the old banana skin.
It can take three, the number magical
To get the job done. You and me and him
In degrees of love. Can't rule it out; could
Be the formula. I dance with him but
I love you; he does not know and would
Not care. A breath, maybe, a twist of lust,
Is all. He is my sweet gymnastic friend
And you're my hero, where my footsteps end.

2

I love the simple masculine strut of
You. Spread that peacock tail in fear and lust,
What if I don't take notice of you, love?
No fear. What Darwin said is true. I must
Choose you. You are superb. Show the colours,
Talk about your golf game, how so it is;
I will listen. I am riveted. Oh lover, whatever
You say is fine. Human-divine, your phys-
iology speaks to me in tongues. It's
Not just that, though that's enough. I love your
Whole idiot self, and mine when I'm with
You. Lift up your pinfeathers, my heart will turn
And track with you: wild bird, I am your seed.
Peck me, take me; let me meet your need.

3

I wore the blue dress and you touched my hip;
So did we get to first base? What a mess,
But I don't mind it. No scar your hand left
There, more of a signature, that warm grip
Fleeting, that I feel when I close my eyes.
You had a backpack on; I touched your arm
And ran my hand down, duet in backpack form,
Strange third. Pregnant, reversed, you tried
To laugh it off, big boy, smile and run. But
There's no getaway. Eyes dilate to black,
Quick, turn your back and hide. Sweet jack,
I know your mind. It's mine. So what
Do we do now? I do not know. Nor you.
We wait, we wait, and see it through –

4

I love it when you boast. Do you show off
In bed? Guess there's no need by then. Job's done.
I love the energy and need, epic
Excitement and greed, hero in the hall.
There is no topic too small to bring it on.
Oh subtly sing my praise for getting out
Of bed today, for being this damn cute,
Funny, canny, wise, on time, and strong.
For admitting gallantly when I am wrong,
Though I am mostly right. For pants superbly
Tight. For everything you like about me.
Listen to what I did, me, laconic,
Swift. Listen to what I'll do. Feel the thrill.
I'll do it. Swear. Yes, I know you will.

5

Touchy, touchy, beauty boy. And you say
You have no ego. The slightest hint of
Disapproval and you get plaintive
Or your hackles rise. You don't really
Know what you want from me. Fortunately,
I do. Reinforcement: you've long been short.
You need a constant bath. This phase may pass,
But I don't think so. Fine. Come right back
With a stung retort. Yet women pet you,
Do we not? Why? Not because you're cute.
Because it's what you're looking for. Mama's
Hurt boy cries out, help; helpless, we answer.
No fair, you say, I suffer. I agree.
I hear. Men like you need women like me.

6

Just what is it you were saying again?
Something about Joyce. Wise. I got lost.
Fantasy of creeping round the podium
To suck your cock. Apposite, I recall,
To the topic you were lecturing on.
Bit of a surprise, though. Not what the class
Expects, these things made literal. Pardon
Me. Go on. Can you? I work on two tracks
Well. You? Fireworks, indeed. Snap, crackle,
Pop. White-knuckle grip. How long can you keep
It up? Hmm, a good long time, it seems,
You sexy fuck. Two minutes, the bell will
Ring. Think you can last? End of the service:
Let it go, what the hell. *Nunc dimittis.*

7

These are old problems, old as Augustine.
He said we must have faith in things unseen:
Believe our friends befriend us; lovers love.
We cannot know, because between us lies
The great distance of mind from mind, galaxies
Apart. Yet from across the room I feel
Your heartbeat quivering on the air.
I start when you come in, involuntary.
You disturb the air and I'm inspired
By your chemistry: I breathe you in,
As real and clear as oxygen. *Fort, da*
Is bridged in juice. Even if you stand aloof,
Faultless information loops across our
Space, no matter what Augustine says.

8

I think if I could seduce your hands,
The rest would follow. Maybe just one
Finger. Hands, after all, expand the world.
They type, they eat, all the fun stuff. They reach
Out in that first light touch, tentative on
The shoulder, small of the back, in passing.
Not too much at first, small overcoming.
Sensitive to skin and to permission.
And the moment at which assent is given
Is crystal clear. We always know when that
Circuit is closed. Invisible, electric motion
That unites two systems. Digits become nodes;
Information flows faster than we can trace
Or calculate. Hear what my fingers say.

9

Husband me, hell yeah, I am twice proven,
Two beautiful children. I am good earth.
Get on your knees and till me under heaven;
My womb's been lived in and it longs for birth.
Score a furrow, chances are I'll farrow;
Tamp down the seedling once I've been well harrowed,
Own it, lover. They say third time's the charm.
Oh baby, it's time to buy the farm.
Play dirt, pay dirt, pray dirt, let me lay your
Firstborn in your arms and see you weep.
Let my lips spill forth thy praise, fierce heart;
The truth will gush out bloody. Do not sleep
Tonight. Wake with me, take me, do not wait.
The day will come it could be all too late.

Of course I've always wanted your body
But really you are a thing of mind.
Ideal, inspired, inspiring, unconfined,
Filled with wish and breath, though not only
Those. Suspicious of your flesh, keeping it
In line because it's hurt you in the past.
Therefore suspicious also of mine, alas,
That I might hurt you with it, and this
Is possible. Your fears are just and right.
You seek cerebral refuge from past pain,
A place to stand and be a man again
Inside your skull. Police the edge: keep tight
Control, oh prisoner of conviction,
You who were too long the body's victim.

1 1

In the end it would never work, my friend,
Because our braveries are not the same.
You are the fighter and I the lover:
Put us together, we'd be the perfect man.
You fought the coffin from the cradle
And I sought to heal the clan. These are not
Battles that we won. They're not susceptible
Of winning. Yet those who fought for everything
See no point in giving. You see me speak
The truth, tough, as you would do. I see
You do the same and my brave heart, it breaks.
Such are the paths the different heroes take.
I will see you leaning on a broken spear
And you will say, what are you doing here?

Portrait of the artist as a young jock:
Volleyball, was it? Hockey? I dunno,
Lacrosse? Soccer, whatever. Might get stopped
In football. I fear you'd be crushed pronto,
Ack – but here you are, uncrushed, and on
Miraculous form, figuring out
What I say, play by play, wordlessly.
There's some script you read, as you bob and weave,
Wholly, fluidly, an athlete of mind
That gets me every time. How do you do it?
You bring me, precise and strong, into
Your body's song, increase my fluency.
Fleetingly. When we cease to move, it's gone.
So whatever game we're playing, bring it on.

1 3

The dancing writes itself into me hard;
It shows up dark; the bruises stretch for days.
I wake with hands upon my thighs, clear marks
Of separate fingers, carved in like Braille –
Except made up of touching, not to touch.
Here is that lift, that spin, that crawling on
My knees. The hard line of your shoulder – the crutch
That lifted me – it made my right arm bleed.
Under the skin, the message, see? I read
It like one punch drunk, the words it left: I flew.
Not far and not forever, but I did:
Yesterday, with you. Everything I knew
Fades beside these bruises. They're the truth.
Until I can grow feathers, they will do.

14

It's like dancing with one of the Elgin
Marbles, just more bouncy. Though one of those
I could not lift, and you I can, if you
Help me. You make a classical impression
In both look and motion. A perfect faun.
Ideal in the proportion of the face
And graceful frame, exuberant Greek curls,
Fine furry legs for carrying off the girls.
In your movement like a frieze: straight back, bent knees.
Sidewinding spiral, geometric form.
Emergent, joined. A bas relief, but free.
Architectonic agent: how can that be?
Mysterious caryatid holding up
The door, yet going through it evermore.

Your blue period's more fun than Picasso's.
You roll and hurl and swarm with yours, frisking
Around with that big blue ball. It rolls
Away: the sentence just won't end. Risking
Ellipsis, beautiful man, you …
Dive and twirl and ride across the floor.
Again, again. Unselfconscious, though
You know I'm watching. You perform
The circus of yourself, *saltimbanco*
Of this life, pure form uncensored. No sad
Clown with the lights down, no azure show,
Regret, calliope horse entrapped.
No distance between what you think and mean:
The thing itself. No interrupt.

16

You put me in mind of a horse I used
To ride, name of Cosmo. Feisty, upright,
Not very big, part Hackney, so built
For the road. We got on like a house
On fire. In retrospect I realize
Many of my best friends were horses.
They don't talk much. Big relief. Strong silent
Types, communication brief. Nothing worse
Than a chatterbox after a while, if
You're one yourself. Wonderful to shut up.
Cosmo was a joker, an equine wit.
He did the unexpected, made me laugh.
Snort, stamp, half-rear, grouchy in the morning;
Powerhouse who nips you without warning.

1 7

Make me thy lyre, Shelley said.
But I play you like an instrument.
I'm the ecstatic one, yet you're the lyre.
Maybe you call me out by accident,
A freak effect. You're my marionette
Today, beautiful and loose, click, clack,
As you comply. And yet you fly – you're free –
You carry me. I hold the strings; you sweep
Me off my feet so we are travelling
Across the sky, I am a dead leaf thou
Mightest bear – silly dear, you just don't know
This stuff, do you? Yet all the shapes you make
Are clear. From you the wind blows true,
Without desire. I am the liar.

18

People speak of the problem of three: you,
You, me. I have found it quite otherwise.
I'm surprised at the strain on the mood,
The cost of one line going through
To one object. Thus when I'm mad at you,
I can just redirect, and continue on:
Fawn on the machine, machine-gun the faun,
Addressee switcheroo. Keeps things toned down.
Nobody needs six hundred complaints
When three hundred will do. It reins in my stride
And shows each of you in a better light,
When you alternate crossing the finish line.
While I am the third who walks always beside
And gets the last word across her heart's divide.

19

A hundred twenty; two hundred eighty;
How many do we want? How close the zoom?
How tight the data map? Cleave to the psyche;
Widen to the world? Leave in the bitchy
Breakups; take the long view? Let charity
Imbue the wider spread? Immediacy
Or wisdom, which to choose? Why both, you say,
Reader far away, unhurt, if not unmoved.
Accurate and cruel. I don't dispute your
Mastery. I'm what you mean by love.
Posterity's the judge who says, I will
Punish you for things I did not do.
I will admire you even as you lose.
You lack. You lie. You help us choose.

Mmm, that t-shirt looks as good on as it would
Off. Yes, well-washed cotton, soft to the hand.
I used to sell this stuff. I know it well.
Now I'm selling something else. Time will tell
How much you're buying. Meanwhile, I do not stare
As you sit not quite innocent in that chair,
At ease, well pleased, happy to be admired:
The male animal. You bask and smile,
Ask me to tease and praise you. I comply.
You are not as complacent as you seem.
Your wounds can still be seen and you know I
See them. So, casual, you keep coming by
To show me they're still green, still gory,
So I don't close the book and end the story.

2 1

I saw you through the glass, momentary,
Twining up some cable, busy, as I passed.
I thought: why does this farce persist?
Why can I not suppress the interest
That your face excites, even the line
Of your shoulder turned away?
No one has anything to gain. My mind
Is resolute, and yet – my eye is fast,
So fast. To you it runs like lightning,
Shivering to the rod: uninterrupted,
Coursing to its highest god. Blazing in
Its assumption that you are safely
Grounded, even as I know that this love's
Unfounded. Every time, astounded.

2 2

Did you know all forty-year-old women
Come equipped with a studfinder? Even
The dykes, *mutatis mutandis*. Yes, it's
A special feature. Kind of a last-ditch
Evolutionary thing, find a partner
Before you die. Use all your wiles to find
The last man. Erect that solid wall, all
Square, against the end. Advantage of mind
Over flesh. Young chicks don't have it all.
In fact, they're often moronic. Why do
Guys come to us, perplexed, balls in a knot,
Not knowing why? We have the follow-through,
You see. We also lust, we want, we stamp
In our image. *Imprimatur*: a man.

23

Are you a shower or a grower?
Wow, that is the question. What have you got
Right now, in a state of relaxation?
For whom does it all hang out, under
What motivation? Some men give their all
To all, some respond to invitation.
In an extended sense, of course, it's rich,
Suggestive of the way in which you live
In time, whether still upcoming or arrived.
Are you best now or later? When's the peak?
Hidden reserves, or pistol without sheath?
You look like a grower to my eye.
Delicate flower both of cock and mind
Spectacular potential but a wee bit shy.

.

24

A rival makes for value. That's why
Natives are useful: they mark the place to steal.
Just the same with art: we recognize
The muse. Why re-invent the wheel?
Most muses are re-used. Just like with you:
I saw you dance with your first master
And realized then what I was after.
Through others' eyes we see the truth.
And you, my friend, came pre-admired
By a rival poet. And man, you let
Me know it, every time we met: that
You'd been had and came already wired.
A rival is a thing we fear and taunt
Even as he shows us what we want.

2 5

Foster parents of the precocious child,
Aren't we, my friend? We've not yet met
Yet I know you so well, first tamer
Of the wild heart. At least, you made a start
On that rude grammar. And who would want to
Smooth it over wholly in its power?
Not you, or I. We who love the lover.
Who see his God's not gone and won't be, ever.
In whom his pain and wrath create desire
And so we shape and save and mentor
From lapse to lapse so that he may better
Himself, and us, in his Promethean hour.
Ah, these myths, they stretch our ethics. It's
Quite difficult to raise an epic.

26

Impending funny moment. Hard to think
What to compare it to. Like meeting the
Sperm donor? Inexact. Now the other
Imaginary parent shows. He slinks
In to take his place and tips his hat.
He knows his role, I'm sure, and can guess mine.
Face to face we stare over our errant child.
We can't speak frankly while he's here, the blessed
Heir. Or are we rivals breathing each other's
Air? God forbid. Neither is cut out for it.
We anxiously admire our joint prize,
Exchanging glances from the corners
Of our eyes. Our boy is fine. A miracle.
Born of parents purely theoretical.

27

Sequence is not important. I have two
First memories of you. One is of your
Face laughing in the shade of a stairway,
An intense flash, as beautiful as fake
But true. I hear your running feet as you
Look back, Eurydice. I am laid low.
Also I see you dance, do a straight-arm
Charge across the floor, someone before
You, hapless, yielding place. Helpless
In that toil of grace advancing like a
Rapier, I say to the teacher who
Stands near: God, where did you find him?
I know, I know, she says, and nods and grins.
Two points at which the story of you begins.

28

Experimenting with unusual grips
I get the soft gift of your equipment
Resting briefly on my leg. These liquescent
Parts of us that we hide away, as if
Shameful, are just in another state,
One not quite solid. Breasts that we have to
Pour into cups to carry, hanging
Testicular sacs, ridiculous, they
Pose a challenge to the rest of us.
We are not all hard, all made, cooked to
The max. Just as our breath is gas, so too
Are we these trembling yolks, delicate
Skinned fluids. Amid your solid strength
Is change of state, always being born again.

Cuddle me gently and don't talk, dumb jock.
Quietness is a boon. From you I learn
The peace that comes into the circle
Of your arms, untermed, while you return
To the imaginary womb, land
Before time that lives beneath my skin.
Not so much get it on as in. Your hand
Cherishes my back and your face wears its zen;
I don't need to see them with my head tucked
Into the curve of your neck. The world moves on.
We stand and breathe. Among the things that are are we,
Beautiful and strange, as indeed is being.
Let the atoms of our bodies dance. Say nothing.

30

Do me to know what way thou wilt I bend:
For unto thee have I raised up my mind.
So said he, Wyatt, love of any who
Have sense. So I will dance for him with you
With brave and faltering grace. With roughness,
Never finding any end, without
Perfection. Our feet will tend to resist
The tyrant death, while knowing that
It cannot happen. Into you my breath
And touch suffuse and my wit follows.
Dance me, my Lord: now my chest is hollow.
My heart's gone out and wreathed with yours,
Twice beating, strong. Godless we face our fall
Together, losing, finding, losing all.

3 1

My soul in thee hath more desirous trust
Than hath the watchman looking for the day –
Wyatt's line, I only change the addressee.
I hate the morning but I know just what
He means. That you will be there exactly
When I need, unexpectedly. Rock steady
Comes the dawn you want, and yet you wait
To see. Even so you dance with me.
They say sheep don't know the dawn until
It's proved each day in light. They sleep without
Desire, wake from eternal night. No doubt;
No joy fulfilled. You rise to rules, and fall:
I and the world obey. We listen to
Newton's laws that what will be will be.

3 2

Teach me thy will, that I by thee may find
The way to work the same in affection:
Wyatt, again. Third time pays for all. Bind
Me thus loose; you choose my direction,
Pass it through your veins and let it bleed
Into me. Let me recline in your
Volition; let us be joint at need,
Responding to the time. Forever
Isn't now. I've never been. Have you?
Contingency's the thing conditions us.
Bend my arm and torso, sinuous
In line with yours, with yours. Do
Me to move as you move yourself, my limbs
In your decision, effortless.

33

Radical submission, you say, is what
You offer. To me, as your avenging
Mother? So you will beg and scream and weep?
No – you mean as the floating leaf
On the breast of the moving stream,
The freedom gained. So you surrender
With no pain upon the midnight of broad day,
Right here, with me. Now in this dance,
Under forces huge and adamant.
A world is in a person, with a will.
Uprooting us to move is radical.
Powers move us that make the planets spin,
Whirling up our dust, gargantuan;
Delicate as dew upon leviathan.

34

Take me with you into quietness. Enclose me,
Never let it end. Time is elastic;
It extends between the digits' change
Up through your back that bends, your ribs that spread,
Into the infinite. I follow you
To the beginning, to the moment when
All things invent themselves. Your blood flows through
Me; I arrest. Then I am born again.
I you, you me, wings sweep from our joint spine,
New creature, endless, seamless cherubim,
All eye, all flesh, all touch and sword combined,
Piercing the real. The garden gained and lost
And made all in the instant of our trust
In every atom of our dancing dust.

35

They flee from me that sometime did me seek.
This does not stop them seeking. Still they flee.
A greater distance to overcome means
Greater love. Carrot hanging on the stick
Way out in front, where steps cannot close
The gap. It's not just me. No one wants
The game to end. As if reluctantly
They return again, all nonchalant
With small, innocent questions. Woe is me,
I need to know. Riddle me this. See
What I do. Praise me. Tell me it's okay.
Arrest me, fascinator. Stop me in my tracks.
Put your interpretation on my facts.
I come close, then run. It's my startle reflex.

36

Skittish, aren't they, these young men? You'd think
We were going to bite them. Nibble on them,
Maybe. But they're not ready. Push and they blink.
They're so very serious. Again
And again they creep to the brink. Then they
Scream and run away. It is quite funny.
Not to them, of course; to precipitate
Divorce is not their plan. Ah, so manly
As I am, I am a threat. She'll just go
Crazy. Lose her head, as after all
I am the bomb. Tick tick. They hang around
With casual aplomb. They work so
Hard, in truth, but rarely to get over
Themselves. If they do, well, here's the clover.

37

You are an impossibility trope.
I get it. I'm not an idiot.
And you're the one tantalizing and close,
The unzipped ellipsis, pants always half off
And half on. And me, the addicted,
Zooming around employing you both.
Never say unpaid. It wouldn't be true.
I have paid plenty. Just maybe not you.
I have paid one debt off with another.
I have played mentor and lover and mother
Just as need served. Whose need? Yours. And mine.
Here you're in my world. Yet into my life
You also arrived, both clutching your pearls,
Saying: these are my eyes. Be my guide.

38

I reckon you'd be safe in my house now.
If you were standing innocently round
The barbecue, holding some drink or plate
Would I throw you off the porch and tear your
Clothes off on the lawn, making the party wait?
No, I would not. Thank God. The hostess
Is okay. She has recovered some
Decorum. I no longer think my hands
Would shake taking your coat, not even to
Lay it on the bed. I have come a long way.
Not a whimper would accompany
Our vapid chat about the symphony.
After you'd left, though, I'd feel you in the house
Stirring and scurrying, like the Christmas mouse.

39

I am dancing, talking, multitasking and
I feel you near. I hear your voice; you speak
In passing, wry and comical. You leave
A trail of gold across the cold ceramic floor.
I do not see you leave. My shoulderblades
Calculate the distance to the door. Meanwhile,
I do not stop. I do not drop the ball.
I dance. I talk. Your footprints do not fade.
I'm wise and strong. I ride his back and tear
His hair to make my point. You are long gone.
We roll warm across the vanished glow
Of your trajectory. Only I know it's there.
You cannot help but be magnificent
And it makes all parts of me observant.

40

Oxytocin, meet dopamine. Cuddly
Togetherness, meet cocaine. Crazy,
Invincible, paranoid, may I
Introduce my friend, mister nice guy?
Strange to meet outside my head. Brain facetime
Is quite hard to get. Anything you'd like
To say? Dopamine, don't flex your muscles yet,
Oxytocin's texting, anyway, quite
Unperturbed. He'll notice if you say a word.
OKAY! We got that loud and clear. Oxy-
Tocin, you? Stop nibbling on my ear.
I feel this went quite well. The juice of heaven's
Met the juice of hell, each in his own mortal
Shell. Stare each other down. Your claims are even.

41

Read this: let it blast you backwards through
The plate glass, slo-mo, pure excess. Whoa.
The sheer dumb effect of me and you.
I want more from you than you can know.
More than there is. More than more than.
I assume you'll understand. You won't.
You'll just get mad. I'll take that, lacking
As I am infinite approval,
Endless grace, response commensurate
To my faith. Some kinds of love just rack
Up waste. Your flailing arms and furious face,
I watch them fall. And when you stand again
At least I know you'll take it on the chin
As I stand covered in blood, dripping with guns.

4²

The love of a poet is a bullet.
Who can you ask to take it? You could not.
Can't bear the searchlight's glare, the ripping stare,
Admixture of what's wanted and what's there,
Compressed into a foreign object lodged
In the brain. Invasive love: it causes pain.
People flee it without knowing what it means,
Instinctually. The bloodied shell, falling
From its graze, carries a payload of
The DNA, fine, clean, a better print
Than the original. Such is the hell
Of the beloved, unable to tell
What he might have been, unimpeded,
Unenhanced, out of the pathway of her glance.

43

I suppose it could all come to naught.
I will have nothing to regret. Not
That I won't. But I will have the art.
Powerful, old solace: opens up the heart
Again and again. Not, in the end, a trade –
Lose the lover, gain immortal fame.
What a crock. I wrote all this in love and in
Love I will remain, not just with you. Thin
End of the wedge of sight, the cone of vision;
The beloved leaves the poet's eyes
Stuck open. Luminous, the world arrives
In his wake. It does not go away with him.
Green-branch-bearing-dove, you bring the sign.
Even when you fly, it's still alive.

44

Diminuendo to the subatomic
Level: subtler and smaller than a whimper's
End. Energy whispering and knocking –
Infinite, infinite, in.
Our feet and voices still, yet never gone:
Dancing beyond our ken, beyond our will.
Responsibility no longer mine.
Let the particles quiver in their time
And bless the void. I, myself, am tired.
Infinite partner, I loose your hand.
Manchild whose pain and power paints the sky
From horizon to horizon, lover
Of the mind, in you I loved the world,
Which is far too large for a single girl.

45

I release you into her hands, girlfriend
Fiancée, wife. Slip through my yielding
Fingers without strife. Unharmed but not
Untouched you go to birth your life,
To get the things you need, all the things
To own and be that I cannot provide.
She can, some of them. You will have to
Fill the gaps. That is adulthood. I
Clear the field. I cede the floor. I do not
Want you any more. Not that you're
A broken toy: you are the man I cannot
Have. I don't know how. Go to her.
Be her lover and be well. Me? You
Didn't ask, and I won't tell.

46

Things are slow. So, when the book comes out,
Where will you be? Will you drive cross-country
Through the snow with shaking hands to confront
Me? Get drunk in front of the TV,
The babies squalling upstairs? That's where
I'd put my money down. *So muss es sein.*
Honoris causa you will stay at home.
You will remain yourself, bound by shame,
And love and obligation. Just as did I.
There is no room to live in the airless
Space of the pure mind. I know; I've tried.
There is nothing there but suffocation.
Stoic, you will say: that was not me. Not
What I meant at all. Not what I meant. Oh, but –

47

I've decided that you are a sonnet.
A tensile frame in which I exercise
Myself. Containing, isometric:
You make me strong as I push your limit.
There you are: foursquare, sturdy, linear.
You measure out the world by feet, secure.
The hinging quatrain of your spine meets mine,
Controls our fall, divides our time.
The man who rolls across my shoulder
Without fear. True to the passing moment,
Pure. Who moves my thought from here to there.
Who is wisdom in form, impersonal.
Impersonated. That's a tricky space,
But it conveys the nature of your grace.

48

Curly head lying in my lap as we
Pause in this dance. Don't look up; let my hands
Rest there. From your breath condensation
Dampens my leg. Arms stretch across me.
We are a sculpture by Rodin: maybe
The lovers. So it would appear to outside
Eyes. Our culture's lost the touch, concrete,
Of touching. Our quiet resting sighs
Therefore would read as sex. Maybe they are.
That's fine. No harm. Two people joined
And still: always a sign that stands against
Ruin, even if they sit, or lie entwined.
Sprawl across my knee, lover, dancer, stranger,
Silent elegy of two in danger.

49

Yes, my hands are warm. Hot even, when
I'm well fed. That's twice you've said it, marvelling.
Do you picture them on your belly
On a cold day? In the office creeping
Up your thigh? Why is it of interest?
It seems to be a compliment, some
Fundamental statement. Hmm. Hot mama,
Keep me warm? Snuggle me to your breast?
You'd claim it was pure fact, mere observation.
No, it is pleasurable sensation
And the noting of that pleasure. Put your
Hands on me, purr purr. Warm hands, right here.
From the back of the car, around the seat;
We sit apart. Your warm hands touch my heart.

50

My ass is smarter than your whole body.
Hah funny; also true. Wit beats physique.
In the long run only, love. Now your mystique
And sweetness conquer all, as signs of life
Where these are only records. In the mean
Time – and time is mean, to me at least – teach
My wise ass to dance with you and unlearn
Its pride. Let me not triumph but enshrine
Your ephemeral motion; be not cruel,
But wise. I know enough to know our talents.
They are two and not the same. Let me rhyme
Your habits into time. Oh you oh you my lion,
Lift me onto your golden back, to outrun
Death. Let me let you – let us – outlast breath.

5 1

Saw you dance with my daughter. Opened her,
Sought her, cared for her, brought her out of herself.
She was young and shy; you were old and wise.
Oh if I could have had you then, what could I
Have been? Not a question, love, you can answer.
Brave and unfailingly sweet, you came to meet
Her. You were her teacher, as you were
Mine. Poised between us, equidistant,
On the line. Into the middle, bold, with
A golden heart you leap, lithe stag unflagging.
Why? What do you gain? Just a nagging
Need to be kind? Or to dance, keep that body
Moving? Or is it our deserving?

5 2

It's a bird! It's a plane! It's you throwing
Yourself on your head again, testing
The bouncy floor. You lead your whole
Life on springs, how much more do you need?
Look at you pronking around at speed,
Curly gazelle. You make my hooves split through.
Just look at you, in your splay-legged grace
Fighting gravity for place. You shake
Your mane and buck and roll and slide.
The matted veldt under your feet is wide.
Let me run at your side, king of the deer;
Butt me and chase me for I will not fear,
Gentle heart. Not you, with your painted eye
And silken muzzle, dancing with the sky.

53

I feel it's time for a policy statement.
This is a work of fiction. You who read,
You get that, right? Look at the legal
At the front: believe. It's pure bullshit.
You should never trust what the poet says.
We amuse ourselves in different ways.
Most days I am pure Walter Mitty. My
Relationships are just as shitty as yours.
It's just I have the nerve to lie. I mean:
Can you believe these guys? I wish I could
And I know them quite well. You don't, so you
Can never tell. Alas, it's true
That poets are the worst sort of liars
And yet they keep on finding buyers.

54

Action figures. Yes. We'll need marketing.
Tiny interlocking parts. Look, they dance!
They fuck! They wring their hands! She can
Wrap her leg around her head. And him?
He does handstands. Can they . . . upside down?
They can! Cool. The third, what does he do?
We all wish we knew. Take off his shirt:
He's covered with words and vines. Alert
And wary, he looks round, wood wose. No one
Knows exactly what he sees, primeval mind.
He's anatomically correct, each time,
We find. Ready to roll, but not for fun.
Behind every version of his plastic face,
Unseen, unseeing, a diamond is placed.

5 5

Oh one for whom I bleed, it is Tenebrae.
Christ is blinkered now. The world is dark.
Come to me now. I need your sacred spark.
I have bled out. Lord knows I tried and tried
And there was nothing. Nothing. I will be
As I am, but not tonight. Come to me under seal
Unspeaking, heal me, rip my soul apart.
Unrule me, say not so, revive my heart
In one puncture and blow; not a vacuum
But a seething glow that dries my veins.
Burn me, turn me, enfold me in your wings,
Let them sweep shut caustic on my pain.
Make a new fountain. Let it start again.
Only you can. Bring me to birth, angel and man.

56

The day of your wedding is coming.
My heart will be rent. But it will mean less
Than it's already meant. Entropic,
The system has peaked. Now it's in loss.
The day comes; the day goes. Your life changes
In law, and that's all. Mine, even less.
You'll find that it's drift much more than progress.
The babies will help. They make real claims.
They give the life shape and transcend the remains
Of the past. They will force your hand. Unless
It's been forced before and I doubt it has.
Not by me. I did not use my strength,
Save to hesitate. So I split and re-formed.
And you took the skin and sewed up the gown.

57

Suddenly everyone's wearing suspenders.
My skinny young son, his pants will fall down.
You've got enough there to keep them around
Your hips. I mean, enough where it counts.
And you! It's all painted on, anyway,
What's to fall? Save the women you pass in
The hall, who hope you'll get stuck on a nail
And cause a sensation. Can't blame them.
May the bride who unbuttons yours give you
All you deserve. Let her fingers unfret
You. Ah, let her get you. Remember
I got you before. Where it counts. In the head.
Me alone, so you said. Alternate faces
Of love. It takes two to make braces.

58

Of course I still do entertain the odd
Mental scene in which we tear our clothes off
In the car, but on the whole my love's evolved
You far beyond such mundane things. God's
Toy, not mine, angel on high. So the mind
Protects itself from ruin, through myth's
Slow release. So I save us, jointly,
Me from you, and you from me: with the
Insulating power of poetry.
The wingless originary dove's
Confined to song, and normal life goes on.
Reality springs back into the shapes of sanity.
Angels are far less mad than we. Unliving
And unloved, they need not be.

59

Even fantasy sex inflects to the
Personality. With you it's all about
Permission: what will you accept? This touch
And this, and this, and when will you freak out?
When will you notice that it's me? When will
I break your envelope? Or can you stay
Safe in there and let your body act, same way
You dance? – With you, no chance. Straight in for the kill,
Once you decide. You copulate in mind.
Grasp the nettle, make the symbol gasp, show
Me your mettle, make me proud. Force me to know
The strength of your invention, to desire
Your intention, come with you for the ride.
Worlds away, yet each a prick inside.

60

These poems teach even me. Ah, they feel
Artful, like I'm in control. Like I'm looking
For the right angle: how they'll play in sequence.
I look at them and say, yeah well, hell
With that: what I want's that guy. Really,
What's the problem here? How many bushes
Can we beat? Bullshit about our wishes?
Yet I get caught on words like *pain, dance, angel,*
Sweet and everything changes. It's not just
Me and my desire. Problem of other
Minds. Worse, my lust itself gets refined.
It widens, curlicues and grows –
Takes on things that I don't want to know. Blast.
Poets. Who says I want it all to last?

6 1

Best to have two lovers. Keep everybody
Guessing which one you are addressing,
Including yourself. Adds to the expression,
Which is what it's all about. Shoddy
Work's intolerable. Complexity
Is all. Plus you need the outs – deep breath, sweet,
It isn't you. It's him. It's me. Which one
Are you again? Step over here so I can –
Tell? Ah yes. You. And me. Today. Don't worry,
No one will ever know. Nothing to see
Here, folks, nothing, just move along. All
Asses look the same. Differences are small.
Interchangeable widgets in the end,
Pure function, merely what the muses send.

6 2

The grass did not grow back after last year.
We killed it, dancing. I accept its death.
The winter slept and we as two black bears
Went to our cave and curled up there for months
Dancing in slow spirals. Hibernation's
Done. Skinny with winter's loss we crawl out
To the world again to shed our skins.
We claw each other bare. Our bloody snouts
Rip raised until we're naked. Helpless
And small we're free to alter all. We bring
The spring. Our arms hold up the trees.
Our eyes see blue. Our feet invent new seeds
And drive them into ground with every move;
Sweet is the death that takes its end by love.

63

When I am eighty, love – I'm halfway there
Already – I will remember that picture.
The roll, the legs in the air, the unashamed
Movement through space and time. The way
I rode my nerve, effortless on your frame.
The life so short, the craft so long
To learn: at the halfway mark I turned.
I turned and turned. On the ball of my foot,
Curve of your back, crux of your heart. We spurned
The ground but we were wise and used its force,
The way it pulled us down, entropic, to
Rebound. Laws are huge like love without remorse
Or pain but you must risk the fall. Only when
You give it up do you see mercy's all.

64

Big paws should be ungainly but they're not
On you. They suit your animal. Nice and
Visible, gestural, Picasso hands.
Portrait of the artist as a mountain man,
The village innocent. The virtuous
Second son, who goes out and saves everyone
In the fairy tale because the elder prince
Is a selfish boob. Who worries about his mom.
The better scion whose big hands grip
The nest to peer in gentle. Who leaves
The birds alone. Whose job is not to know
But to support and carry those he loves.
Jaunty axe-bearer from a silver print
In a simpler world that now is spent.

65

Dance, my sweet, extends in time, as does
Human love, ephemeral, unlike rhyme.
Poems make it so that we, unlike,
Can catch each other up. Gorgeous beast,
I mean: you can catch me. Come track me down,
Sometime when I am gone, and say: how she
Loved me, and how lucky was I. I've left the key.
Return with it in your hour of need:
Unlock the belated power of poetry.
Under the leaves of this, the beaten tree
My love observes dendrochronology,
Unfolding slowly, line and whorl
Into your mind, there writing me.
Nested at end inside the boy, the girl.

66

Have you ever seen a grafted tree? They're rare.
I once saw one that bore apples and pears.
It was truly weird and strangely beautiful,
Twice-fruited. Copious, plentiful,
Glorious. Could that be us? Is this
The image I should use? Not ancient
Vice, unnatural growth, nature underneath
The yoke, but free to flower twice, he/she?
Joined at the stock; two bodies, and two sets
Of thoughts? Two lives and yet one energy?
So then, where do I make the cut? You ready?
Breathe, my love, and close your eyes. I throw away
The grafting knife. The job is done. We are
Already one, life slipped into life.

67

Third spring since this began, I am afraid:
Troilus and Criseyde and Diomede.
Hah! Not quite. No siege. Less death. This production
Is low rent. Criseyde does not get laid
But writes the book. God knows she tried, but
Was plagued by hesitations from three sides.
Ever vigilant crocuses deride
All sex but their own, which every time
Works out as planned. They thrust and come into
The womb of air each year, replicating
Themselves by brute assault. Instead, we care
And get hung up on details, to a fault.
The crocus does not write this story, rather
The twining and recurving morning glory.

68

See you and raise you. Raise you like an island
Hove in sight. Raise you like the wind under
A kite. To an angel down from Paradise.
Raise you to the power of the infinite.
All games of chance bore me to death, so
I raise you like a feather on my breath.
No one bets against the gods but fools
And they have nothing else to do, except
Rule nations and shoot to win at pool.
Not so I you. You are the real deal.
I've spun you high on fortune's wheel
Because you deserve to be there, in my view.
And then, seeing what you have become
Just staying in the game, I've won.

69

That was the weirdest thing ever. There you
Were in my kitchen, just like a normal
Person. I did not faint. Informal
Conversation was made. Calmly I cooked
Chicken. The kids ran around, loud. It was
A sitcom, wholly prosaic. Strange
How one man can change, wax and wane like
The moon. A man of mid-height stands in a room.
He has tattoos. No imminent doom
Assails me. Or you, standing there, not
Too fraught, unaware of the terrible
Places you've been in my thought. We sat
Around and talked about regular things
And I kept looking behind you for the wings.

70

Behold the bridegroom who outshines the bride.
Glowing, happy, dapper, bold, I see him
Walking up the aisle in your eyes.
I was not there. I would have cried.
He is the son less broken, who though not whole
Is wise; who earned in pain and now may learn
In joy. Your golden boy. In this love, no shame.
I feel his springing tread as you say his name,
Making his way up, the woman by his side,
To vow his honour, speak his boast and say:
You, I take. Long since taken, you and I
Watch him pace past and give her up the day.
We have had time and will again, in ways
She cannot know, in the sunshine of his gaze.

7 1

Tough and needy, generous and greedy;
Laconic, voluble: smart, moronic.
Swift/slow. Yes/no. Tight control and panic.
Shy brute, child hirsute: sprout that's gone seedy.
Sickness and health; poverty and wealth;
Demography, genetics. Computing
Of aesthetics. Perversely straight, stealth
And display, agreement in disputing.
Universal solipsist, rebel who
Wants the law. Just stroke me and fuck off.
Virtuoso of the introduction.
Parentless, adopted: lucky, screwed.
The man I loved; the man I left; the man
I never knew. X, O. 1, 2. You.

7 2

We're standing at the bar and I'm buying
You a drink; you are rubbing my back.
Anyone standing behind us will think
You are my man, so sure your hand
In its quiet proprietary right.
Little do they know that you, Mr Uptight
Will stroke my spine but rarely meet my eye.
That you reach out without asking why,
Seeking comfort, seeking to comfort me.
Your hand performs its own soliloquy
Divorced from conscious thought. You are only
Mine metonymically. Your hip, my thigh;
Your hand, my side; our clavicles have met
And kissed and understood. Our heads, not yet.

73

I dream of those strong brown hands on my breasts,
Cupping them, holding them up, touch firm
And capable. I dream of your breath
On my neck, smooth inner wrist cross my arm
At the top, knee in the small of my back
As I turn to kiss you. Rotate and glide:
Hand on the sacrum, hand on the thigh,
Closed eye to closed eye, unbroken touch –
A long cycle, improvised. I dream of
Your flesh, of its scent, of its weight, with my
Body's eye, feeling new angles, new lines
Across mine. I'm below; I'm above,
My fingers entwined in that curly head.
I imagine us dancing in bed.

74

What would a kiss be to a man from Mars,
Estranged? Here's a test case: it would be you
Putting your mouth on mine and mine on yours,
Gentle manipulation. Hand slides through
Your hair, slow up from the cervical
Vertebrae. Hand slides down my back and grips
My side. We both lean in, out of true,
Specific gravity becoming one. Hips
Follow lips, surge of testosterone
In shared saliva, flow of pheromones
As our thoracic spines strive to meet and
Twine right through our flesh. Kissing makes amends
For separation. Resuscitation
Works best mouth to mouth. Note his fascination.

75

Wanted you at the beach. Pictured you frisking
Around like a water dog, lean creature,
Wet head sleek. Chasing balls and sliding
Across pontoons, twisting through the air
Off the high board. More or less suspended
For hours on end, with a disarming grin.
Then coming with me out to the middle
Of the black water, past the lifeguards' reach,
To cuddle under the waves, where no one sees.
Our distant heads look chaste but underneath
My legs are fiercely wrapped around your waist
And I feel your core's heat as it emanates
Into mine. You are shivering with cold
And lust as the lake takes us deep into its trust.

76

Silver diver, dive. In the candlelight
You are an otter, lithe, eyes glinting bright
Against the dark. You almost phosphoresce
In the whiteness of your skin. Break the surface
Of my form, like the otter going down
Into the water. Carry the stone of
Your desire to the bottom. Let it go,
Bob up gasping. You know you will not drown.
Let me be the wave you ride with your
Sinuous spine, sweet drifter. Let our pure
Lust meet in the middle, breaking only
The meniscus of our flesh. No lonely
Animals exist but us. Oh, be the
Otter, writhe with me, uncaring, free.

77

You washing your hands at the sink, beautiful.
Saying, I'm trying to know myself better.
I stand behind you, think: let me teach you, you
Silly fellow. Turn round. Kiss me over
This towel. It's moronically simple.
I am one of the things that you want. Two
Squares behind on this tile. Make the move:
Take the queen. Just a few gentle steps
And our bodies will meet. Then you'll be clear
On this point, at least. Each one of your ribs
Knows already, inclining to mine as
You breathe. Exhaling, the truth just gets nearer –
And passes us by like a breeze, a frisson
As you hand me back the now-damp cotton.

78

No, I won't be your mistress. You can be
Mine. We can switch it up like Aphra Behn.
O master mistress of my body's motion,
King of this passing hour's devotion,
Make my every limb a wishbone cracked across
Your knee. Hold me and mold me and then set
Me free. Let us be the prince and princess
Of androgyny. Lend me your strength and take
From me the speed of my thought. Re-trace
Our nervous pathway back in time, down to
The very bottom of our minds. From the base,
Again we'll climb the trees, and hang there side by side,
Rich fruit. Bitch man, buck girl, the two
Who rule as one the undivided world.

79

Here under the moon, we're easily fooled.
Here where the dance of gravity rules,
Contingently we move. Forces impress
Themselves upon us, as did you, creature
Of earth. Not a lowly, aerating worm,
But a buck born pushing on the world,
Slim, timid and strong. More than you knew
To ask, I gave, and so I lose.
My winged one was aloft and gone –
Amen to him on his sky-roads –
But then his shadow fell on you, and showed
Me your beauty turning on the stair,
Dimly illuminated, mysterious, vast
As a mountain in the light I cast.

80

If I am cruel to you, this is the venue.
Not to your face. I can't. You're such a tender beast.
It would be like stepping on a hamster:
I'd be forever haunted by the squeak.
In a poem you can be diminutive
Without shame, a pocket pet. In person,
At my table, though, you deserve respect.
I sit opposite at dinner, listening
To what you say. I strive to let you lead.
I am a wimp and you are truly sweet.
Sweet. The word itself exasperates,
But you do not. Beauty exonerates
Your faults. If I'm angry I lose track.
Tough poet, yeah: with you in sight I suck.

8 1

I praised you steadily for two years
And that frank praise is what you'll take away.
It did not fall on deaf ears. Now you say
"My beauty," unashamed, whereas
Such words had never crossed your lips before,
Nor yet your mind. People of your kind
Do not praise each other. To them praise is
A lie or an embarrassment. They keep score
In other ways, unstated, circumscribed
And mean, hedged round by irony. Praise is
Not flattery. It's praise. Joy that is raised
By beholding, in security,
A worthy thing. My praise recognized
The beauty of your face and made it be.

8 2

There you are half naked in the half light
Of the hall. I stroke your belly as I
Pass by. I want to push you out of sight
Around the corner but it's not the time.
Sigh. Maybe that time will come. Later in
The same place you kneel and grab my legs,
Joke beg for mercy. How much can I take?
A lot. No worries. Negotiate that sin,
My son. That's what you fear, though not the word
You use. Old interdiction. Funny how
Long they take to die. Adultery: absurd
Notion in the non-sacramental now.
Your hands are on another man's wife already:
You haven't been struck dead, just giddy.

83

Men are like dogs. It's what I've always liked
About them. They proceed by sniffing and
Wagging, jumping and flagging. They tend
To wear themselves out. They're easily psyched,
Though brave and tenacious. Their eyes glaze
With desire. They are pleasantly tactile
And want to lick you all over. They seek praise.
Right now I have a spaniel, an Airedale
And a terrier. Each has his merits,
Whether you want fetching, herding or fighting
Ferrets. They will get along, my hounds,
With no discernible bones around.
Though the upkeep gets expensive,
Without them I would be defenseless.

84

When Francesca and Paolo got into
All that trouble reading, before,
Do we know what sides they took, as they pored
Over the fatal book? Like you
And me, I bet it went by antinomies.
She said: Lancelot's the man, too bad
He lost. And he: how can you say such things?
She loved the king, ancient and sad
And wise, and had loved him long. Good woman.
Good woman going wrong, she said
And dropped the bomb and whereupon
He picked it up and they were gone.
Up in smoke. Waking in a fiery haze,
Each said sorry, what did you just say?

85

Butterfly landing softly on my hand;
Hummingbird treading air below my ear
Afraid to land. Hesitant spider on
My collarbone, clinging in silken fear
Of the drop. The quick ant's trace across
My breasts, stopping and starting to the nest.
Sex with you's a picnic, sugar cubes
And tiny, delicate bribes. Under our hips
The grass stems barely bend. Flower heads sway
By radical degrees, while we shed clothes
Slower than trees their leaves. Generations
Of mayflies pass away in glory, moths
Bang the glass and fall down stunned and furry,
But we, never quite started, never stop.

86

You stand naked and invite appraisal.
I appraise you: if you were on the auction
Block, there'd be a bidding war. That's how
Hot you are. I would split myself to fractions
Just for the fun of winning: divide and
Conquer. Then how many times would be our
First? Pretty exciting. You are trembling
With nerves. Moment of truth, past dissembling:
Time for the first jump. When will it come?
Now? Now, or now? There is no whistle.
Just the movement of our blood past
Bone and gristle, near silent whisper.
Hush lover, do not fear. I will come near.
No rejection, not once I've seen your –

8 7

As their breath goes, some still say no. We don't
Believe them. So with you. Oh no, you swoon
And your eyes roll: oh let me go. I won't.
Hotter than sly fucking flaming June
You burn under my hand, pretend
It's all my fault. Oh no, I say, it's not.
See, I release you. Fly the coop. What?
Still here, chicken? No, do not send
To know the score. We'll find you hanging
On the door, windless and choked, alone
Unless you learn to speak the truth, which is
A progress: resistance, overcoming, ease.
The intimate arc, the fountain's jet:
Oh no, oh yes, oh please. Again, again.

88

Well, you know what they say about fauns.
They keep you busy. Priapic. I'm
Feeling for those stubby little horns –
Stand still, will you? Do we really have time
For this? Aren't we going to discuss that show?
Err, no? That pedagogical strategy,
If you'd just peel your hands off of me,
For one minute? Well, really, you know
I've always wanted to have sex in this chair,
On the kitchen floor, on this countertop.
Don't mind me. There's no need to stop. I'm sure
We've missed the meeting. Classicism is
Pressing and pleasure is fleeting. Ah, there.
I can feel your horns through that curly hair.

89

Just let me love you, sweet and deep and slow.
Let us not think. Let us only do.
Lie with me and listen to the rain.
You and me, and me and you; we'll change
All the world's terms to make it safe for us
To be here, temporarily. For just
This hour we will lie down and cease to lie.
We'll extend a brief circumference round
Our bed made of pure mind in which our bodies
Move until we lose the perimeter,
Fail of the edge, and so remake the world
In our image. Let us lie chest to chest
And gasp and weep and sweat, as all men and
Women do, returning to the nest.

90

Curl up with me, lover, and go to sleep.
Burrow into my warmth; watch my cold feet.
Here we are like two mice in a nest,
Small and sweet. After scrambling comes rest.
Sleeping together is harder than sex:
It takes trust, long practice, or luck – or all
Three. Of these, with us, which will it be?
Not long practice, I fear. As we fall
Into bed so we will fall out. But
Not now. Now our bodies are soft and
Relaxed, held by a chemical bond
In the palm of the world. Our eyes shut
Out light. We are foetal and still, yet
Unborn but conjoined in the innocent night.

9 1

Just couldn't do it, could you? No surprise.
I will not laugh or weep, just roll my eyes.
Can't face the myth. Won't do the lineup.
Afraid of the deep maternal surmise:
That she'd be wise to you when you are not,
That she'd intuit part of what you want,
Unravel all your thought and see how tight
It winds around your dick. You go on
Strangling in your pants in that existential
Angst, and she would see. No fool. Mother of three.
You don't want her standing next to me.
So her flight delay is providential.
I hear you, love: let's not do lunch,
Lest your mother follow up her hunch.

92

Close these covers, everybody's heaving,
Sneaking around from page to page, listening
Looking, leaving. How do we make them stay?
Firm annotations – you're going the wrong way?
If you run into him right now, how's that
Going to help? He's a minister of
Providence and you're a cringing whelp.
Wait til it's reversed. That's in another verse.
Reader facilitator, directing
Traffic through. Wait! Do not meet her! She's in
A bitchy mood. Don't drop that lantern,
You silly schnook, unless you really want
To find yourself in a burning book.
Erotic arsonists everywhere I look.

VII

93

No, don't complain to lover A about
Lover B. Not even for the sympathy
Vote. Don't crowd the scene. Nobody needs
To know everything. Certainly you don't.
As lover A's role has atrophied
Best play it safe with lover B. Preserve
His ego, which is none too secure.
Right now he's got another girl. He feels
He's got somewhere to jump and so he will
If spooked. Just slowly let him work out
The rules. He does not see his tender heart
As part of a collection. Only you do.
Gentle, gentle with the touch. Let him be free.
Only you need feel the repetition.

94

It's possible to make a moral compass
Of your dick, if you fuck the right people.
One that will point you right, help you to think.
Not as a separate thing, an exercise
In overcoming. Intrinsically.
Sex is like speech: easily cast away,
Pearls to swine. Fine. Okay. Some happy swine.
Unhappy you, after a while. For pearls,
Like words, just roll loose and disperse,
Uncatchable, without connecting strings.
Fucking is not pure sound; it's verse.
Sex makes great sense. It's not a stupid thing.
Treat your dick with the respect it deserves
And you'll be conversing with the smarter girls.

95

I say rude things about your current girl
And you, the cat, come back. Petty and cruel:
She and I aren't the same size in any way.
You know this fact. You make a few
Jokes about your dick and glance as I react.
I let it pass. Less would be immoral.
It's not a lovers' quarrel. What I've had
From you she could not get. Of course, my pet,
I will hold your hand, stamp the endeavour
Of your pants with my approval. Just til
You're on your feet. I'll let it be.
You twine about my legs so anxiously,
Purring, twitching your tail, wholly
Misunderstanding my betrayal.

96

She's already feeling tentative, love,
When I'm around. The smugness is gone.
She sees the problem now: what you have done
Is assimilate her into your system,
Which includes me, and you do not intend
To change. In the first rush of dopamine
She thought you'd switch midstream. But no.
The moment she's away, unhesitatingly,
You come to me, without a stretch, even
With relief, in perfect probity.
Poor little bitch, she fights the sea of your sweet
Nature that knows not itself, nor me. Yet,
Keeping us apart, you enjoy all three.

97

I came to dance and show you that I did not care.
With him and her and him. I felt you quivering
With desire and fear. Your eye on me was deep,
Dark and considering, even though she was there.
She, about to leave, the girl, naive but knowing.
She, who should have had you undivided, mourning.
But she did not. You scarcely touched her and she watched
Me with haunted eyes. You do not know how cruel you are,
My love, my prize. How in your indecision all
You do is use. You think that a light grip leaves room
To move, keeps everybody free. Not so. You choose
These poor young fools who cannot hold you as you stall
Your choice, avoid the one who will more than suffice.
Fleeing your love, you hurt those whom you kind of like.

98

Among primates sex is never free. We
Are not mayflies; we live too long and need
To reckon precedence and succession.
You are the junior male who wants his seed
To count yet who is bound by the tribe's rules.
You stand next to me; you stare at me deep;
You invite my touch and eat my food.
You want to be my mate and indicate
It's so by subtle signs, if things should change.
In the power stakes, it's true young men
Are ostracized. Their semen leads. They spend
It on young girls more disenfranchised than
Themselves, gaining strong offspring but less love
Because they failed when push came to shove.

99

There's a poem by Seamus Heaney –
Knocks up the wife apologetically,
Worries about being imperially
Male. Dear me. All that power, what can he
Do? It's a conundrum, through and through.
How to be a man, and not imperious?
What to excise, what might remain: the strain
Is serious. Humility is dull, it's true.
Far better still to fight, and lose. You keep
The drama then. For some of us love men,
And poets, too. They're no use with their feet
Shot off. In you, sometimes, I think I see
The answer. You come back, brave, not knowing
That you fought, or that I am still the boss.

Retreat. From what am I retreating?
To hie me to this little cabin on
The beach? To cross water? To preach wisdom
To the birds busy eating city garbage?
To beat this poor book into shape? No, to wait.
For your visit. This modest space, with you in it,
Complete. The circle closed, for after all,
You brought me here. Ten paces wall to wall.
I have a house at home. I am never alone.
This is not my bed. Its sheets are white.
Let us go dance on the beach at night
And feel the cooling sand between our toes.
See me in a place I do not own, so I am free.
Bathe me in your sweat. Retreat, retreat.

101

Man is his own best friend. At least, you are.
So you have been trained, in a simulation
Of independence. You talk a good game
About empathy but in the end it's far
From your M.O. You carry your own bones.
From time to time you'll carry mine, or hers,
But soon you're drawn back, sniffing round the hole
Where yours are buried. Your pains, your concerns,
Your nuggets of shit or gold. The oldest
Ones are valued most, those worried bare.
Dogs love themselves as they are told, in fear.
They hold onto things lest they disappear.
They don't believe in object permanence
Or that others live and love over the fence.

102

Close a door, love, you'll never know what is
Behind it, or how many more there are
Leading from that room. Small decisions
End up bigger than they seem. Some doors
Come but once and then they're gone, be they
Bottlenecks or nodes, narrowing or branching
Wide. People defend obscure positions, draw
Their own sacred lines. Doors are in short supply.
A future can depend on one handle's turn.
Hesitate and find you've lost all you earned.
Untrue that as you close one, another
Opens. Rattle as you will, the latch is
Broken. Tire in the labyrinth,
Say no. Walls dissolve, leaving you alone.

103

One size fits all fits few that well. Me, never,
In the end. I am too tall. A basic
Truth. I should have guessed it would be true of you.
You cannot stretch to my proportions, though
I commend your flexibility. It
Bends to her and her and me with equal
Grace. Enough to dance us all around the place.
But now our elbows all are showing through
Your carapace. Let me be the first to
Walk away before you are threadbare.
Preserve your strength, preserve your curly hair
For others' use. Least I can do.
Let your fabric relax, snap back to mold
Another body and reveal its gold.

104

I have to fight the impetus to wish
Your plane would crash. You in a foreign
Country admiring her ass: the prospect
Makes me mad. Let the bodies hurl and twist,
Crisp, burning through the freezing air. Except
The children there. Except the virtuous
Women, abused and strong. Except the men
Who never have done wrong. Except the flight
Attendants and all the other staff.
Who's left? Just you and the terrorists.
You kneeling in the aisle, eyes downcast.
No, love, fly on with your wings intact.
I cannot wish harm to one hair of your head.
That trivial bitch, let her die instead.

105

Magnanimity's a virtue we
All hate. It's out of date and it requires
Hierarchies we despise. Yet it aches.
Virtue is born in pain. We may
Reject it when it comes but it gets us
By the thumbs and, like labour, it remains.
The virtue of the master to the slave:
What other virtue can a master have?
A true master denies her mastery. She
Does what she can to keep people free
Of her own power, knowing it is there,
And great and to be shared, judiciously.
True love's true objects: they can walk away,
And the soul, stretching, says, okay.

106

Best thing that never happened to you, sweet pea,
Was me. And I did not transpire, for your
Lack of desire. Best is a hard word,
Perspectived, arrowing, replete
With judgement: best for you, or me?
I stand by best: the you that could have been
Was a beautiful idea you could not see
Or realize. I will not let it rest,
The fantasy, of finding inside you
Someone like me. Self-love, indeed,
The questing kind, that seeks in a foreign
Body the same mind. We wish to meet
Our equals: bold and tremulous, young, old.
Our best selves are the ones that we can hold.

107

I'm not going to hurt you, except for today.
Today, when your eyes alight on this page.
Today I will do it deliberately,
As the price of art. I know there's no way
You can answer, no way that will stick.
No one will hear you; your accent's too thick.
Unlove me, unfriend me. You can break my heart.
That is your freedom, and the price of art.
I'll do it, my love. I don't care what you say.
This is my legacy. All the bills, I have paid.
I wrote down each word though I was afraid.
I accepted rejection out of fair play.
I made you more beautiful. I made you more smart.
And you made me great. It's the price of art.

108

Let's say I replace you with three acrobats
And a strongman twice your size. That leave you
Flat or feeling high? Irreplaceable,
Or left behind? Either way, the show
Goes on. My new menagerie will
Occupy your place, my time and help to form
The next big thing. Next time I'll be
Not a lover but a circus freak,
A contortionist with all the skills I've learned.
A hypnotist with a dowser's wand,
Unerring finder of the needy heart
That craves attention but holds itself apart.
Let's see what happens to the next anointed.
Poets' hearts are always double-jointed.

109

I've given you something very profound.
It'll take your whole life to figure it out:
All the nuances, all of the doubt
And the thought and the love. The whispering sound
Of my heart will still beat in your ears
When I'm gone. No one ever again
Will do this for you. No one can. Your life
Will extend in your kids, with the one
That you choose for that task. Precious, common
Gift that cannot be outclassed. But it can
Be outgunned. Listen. I am the one
Who's defined all you could be, even past
What is true. I made the best you. Now a
Million more minds can see the job through.

VIII

110

There is no more powerful desire
Than the desire to have a master.
Not whips and chains, but aspiration,
The kite's hard pulling lines against the sky.
Oh master, take my hand, secure me
As I rise. Immure me; set me free.
Place me at saving risk and organize
My needs, though never tell me why.
Show me the patterns plain: let me buy them
With pain. Give me something pure to leave
Behind. Hold me and let me go; guide
My arc, string to my bow. Be the brave
One I outgrow, who accepts the final blow
And looks after me as I, wheeling, fly.

111

Here is the other side: to be partner
Without being master is its own reward.
It calls for tact in action. It is hard,
But from it love can grow, maybe farther
Than the love of slaves. To keep the whole
In motion is the trick, a series
Of tiny swerves. Momentum
Is the master then, which both partners serve,
Transcending the pace of one, broken and hectic,
Into two gracious forces isometric.
Share my weight; together we are great.
We yield and prevail, wielding our matter.
Constrain me, contain me in a shape that never
Stops; I'll do the same. We'll fall forever.

1 1 2

Mastery is continuous beginning,
Admitting you will be mastered in
The end. It is the slow abandon
Of desire to be master. Never think
It goes. Not wholly. Nor should it so.
Rather, you hold abandon in your hand,
In tension, like an empty bag to catch
The wind. Release it clear into the flow,
You lose its edge, everything that
You can know, or teach. To preach being
Is the oldest joke, and yet it must be done.
By someone. When the vaunted bag is flat
And lies windless in your grasp, that is the test –
What do I let master me, when the world's at rest?

1 1 3

I need an exit strategy. I could
Keep this going into infinity
And go utterly mad. Stop giggling.
Not funny. Get me out of this shit.
What I need is something definitive,
That never says maybe. I know: a baby.
All demand, all the time, really knows I'm
Alive. Who needs constant protection.
Whose love is simple, voracious, infectious,
Unfeigned. Doesn't doubt; doesn't blame.
Who is worn inside till due time, and then
Pops out to acclaim, and lets me deflate.
Who thinks I'm great. Who looks at no other.
One to whom I am truly the mother.

114

Time impinges from all sides: it is the speed
With which things hit you. For what else is speed?
Speed is expense, expanse, and even such
Is time – velocity that takes in trust
Our life, converts it straight to dust. Yet it
Follows from our consciousness. *Edax rerum*:
That is us. As we are eaten, so we eat.
Tempus fugit – from whom should it flee
If not from us? We who mark the space
Where starlight falls and fails, the central
Registrable void? The final feller
Of all trees? The trouble makers of
Reality, whose all-pervading
Fear makes all things perish, and so be?

1 1 5

We think love can beat death and entropy.
It can't. Best you can do is have it age
And change with you, capably. Holding
A new penny in your hand doesn't make
You any younger, and only richer
By one cent. The youth and beauty of
Another does not mean yours is not spent.
What did you buy with yours? Of that love,
What is left? What interest has accrued?
And how much would you lose, only to
Start again with a single penny? Not
Even yours, but merely lent? A sum
So small you hardly see it in your palm,
Just a glint for which you would trade all.

116

Funny what we take for proof. What systems
Won't admit of truth. Not when the stakes are high.
All that time dancing with you, and I
Believed my flesh, so far as to exclude
Reason. Now, by comparison I need
A small blue strip before I can concede
I am with child. Though my body's certain,
It will not satisfy my mind. A baby
Is forever. You were not. That much I
Think I always thought. Irrelevant, it falls
Away, and gravid, I am left in line
At the office, waiting for the expert sign.
Lasting truths demand corroboration.
Desire is its own elaboration.

I have loved the two of you as men love God:
Father and Son. This is not news. We who
Have lived long enough make every muse
From scraps of what we knew. So is God
Love. He is not small, being a composite
Of all roles deep and cherished. So I have loved
You as neurotic and artistic, forthright,
Ferocious, meek, as vain and unselfconscious,
Strong and weak. As God has been the lover
Of the lonely heart, so have I made you
Out of broken parts to love me whole and plain,
My monsters twain. Though God's not true,
I learned the process of his love from you:
How persons out of persons can accrue.

118

Sometimes you get what you want, the baby
Is laid to rest. Squalling and fret is past.
Then in its sleep the baby turns to stone,
Becomes a dumb cherub or a garden gnome
An ornament that you can walk away from.
Release the bowstring, the bow again becomes
A tree growing in the ground where it was born.
Metamorphosis abounds, and it can   .
Work both ways. Latent energy remains
In forms. The tree will bow and sway
Windless and people think the statue creeps
From night to night. But you, at last, are free.
Others may walk in the quiet park and see
Spent passion transposed into scenery.

119

The day will come, you'll be two retired
Muses, angry, smug, confused, nostalgic.
You'll be those two old guys I knew
Yelling at each other, two feet distant
On adjacent porches. Man, they were obscene.
The air was blue. That'll be you two.
I will have checked out long ago. Remain.
That is your task. Take me with you when you go,
But stay. Worry about your prostates,
Contribute to your RSPs, discuss
Global warming. Go on, age and fuss.
Live on inside this text, just as you must.
Put up your feet. Look back in noble trust.
And I'll be with you every time you take a piss.

120

You fish the fish or you fish the water:
Two schools of thought from *The Compleat Angler*
And two theories of love. In one you chase
The elusive, sliding fin of one you see.
In the other, no, you lie in wait and
Watch one endless ripple's grace until
The shadow comes. In both you may lose bait.
Hard to say which takes more perseverance.
The third option is to be the river.
The fish are fully compassed round; they breathe
You in and can't escape. Eventually
You find their lithe shapes all the same: they quiver
Through you and are gone. And you remain,
Quiescent in your banks, whispering: never.

ACKNOWLEDGMENTS

Thanks to the Ontario Arts Council for an in-progress grant to support this book, and to Artscape Gibraltar Point and the Banff Centre for enjoyable and productive residencies. Thanks to Carolyn Smart, a swift and unerring editor; Jeffery Donaldson, for great patience with the project; Karen Schindler, for the chapbook; Mark Abley, for opening the gate; Lesley Wheeler, for reading the whole thing; and to Stuart MacKinnon, Tristanne Connolly, Danila Sokolov, and Scott Straker, early readers and advisors.